THE GRAND
FAILURE

THE GRAND FAILURE

*The Birth and Death of Communism
in the Twentieth Century*

Zbigniew Brzezinski

COLLIER BOOKS
Macmillan Publishing Company
New York

Collier Books
Macmillan Publishing Company
866 Third Avenue, New York, N.Y. 10022
Collier Macmillan Canada, Inc.

Epilogue first appeared in the Winter 1989 issue of *Foreign
Affairs*.

Library of Congress Cataloging-in-Publication Data
Brzezinski, Zbigniew K., 1928–
    The grand failure : the birth and death of communism in
the twentieth century / Zbigniew Brzezinski.—1st Collier
Books ed.
        p. cm.
    Reprint. Originally published: New York : Scribner,
c1989.
    ISBN 0-02-030730-6
    1. Communism—History—20th century.
    2. Communism. I. Title.
[HX40.B76   1990]
335.43'09'04—dc20   90-1510   CIP

Macmillan books are available at special discounts for bulk
purchases for sales promotions, premiums, fund-raising, or
educational use. For details, contact:

    Special Sales Director
    Macmillan Publishing Company
    866 Third Avenue
    New York, N.Y. 10022

First Collier Books Edition 1990

10 9 8 7 6 5 4 3 2 1

Printed in the United States of America